Practice-Building for Coaches Series

Discover Your Niche

with the GEMS™* System

Marcia Bench

*Generating and Executing a Marketing System – that Works!

Discover Your Niche
Published by High Flight Press 2003

Library of Congress Cataloging-in-Publication Data:

Bench, Marcia
        Discover Your Niche
        / Marcia Bench
        ISBN 0-9724955-6-8
        1. Coaching 2. Consulting 3. Marketing 4. Entrepreneurship

Printed in the United States of America

TABLE OF CONTENTS

Introduction

If you're reading this book, then you either are – or would like to be – one of the thousands of people who are entering the exciting (and relatively new) field of coaching. Coaching is in turn part of a larger movement of millions of so-called "infopreneurs" who are creating businesses that gather, disseminate, teach, or otherwise pass along to others information that is valuable to the consumer. Dan Pink, author of *Free Agent Nation,* states that this segment of the U.S. population – "microbusinesses," temporary workers, business owners, and others who fall outside the category of full-time employee for someone else – are now the largest single segment of the U.S. labor market. Some 32 million people are already working this way in the U.S. alone; maybe now is the time for you!

But for any coach to realize success, he/she must give careful thought and planning to the type of services to offer, the customers to whom to offer them, and what is unique about his/her services versus others.

This book is the second in a series of three designed to help coaches (and by inference, other infopreneurs) navigate the often confusing waters of launching their practice, defining their brand, and filling their practice using techniques specifically proven to work for information-based businesses. Each is used as a textbook for a 12-week teleclass at Career Coach Institute (see www.careercoachinstitute.com for details). These books draw on my nearly 20 years of experience working with people just like you, in both my capacity as a former attorney, as a business consultant, and as a mentor coach. I know it's not easy – but if you know in your heart that there's a "better way," I want to help you bridge that gap from the conceptualization of your dream to its realization. And since I am an infopreneur, too – now in my third business venture – I can personally relate to many of the struggles you are facing – and will in the future!

Of the three volumes in our Practice-Building Series, this is the most "hands-on." To get maximum benefit from this book, please do not just read the content. Instead, as you read one section, please go to the workbook in the back and complete the exercise that goes with it. That way, when you finish the book you will have the foundational pieces of your marketing plan in place. And by continuing to volume 3, *Fill Your Practice,* you will know how you need to apply the tactics presented there to create the unique brand and serve the target markets that you have defined here.

We look forward to supporting you on your journey!

> Marcia Bench and the staff of
> Career Coach Institute and High Flight Press

1: Marketing: the Foundation for Success

What is marketing? If you had to define it, what would you say? Please write your definition below:

Marketing, as we will define it here, is basically *the means by which you communicate to others (directly or indirectly) who you are and what you do.* ("You" meaning your business, your service.) It is "positioning" yourself and your business in the marketplace. It is different from *selling,* which follows effective marketing and constitutes *the interaction (again, direct or indirect/virtual) with a specific individual client/buyer through which they purchase your product or service.*

Notes:

Why Marketing Matters: 3 Key Lessons

When I first entered the world of professional business services over 15 years ago, I knew nothing about marketing. What *seemed* to be happening was that a constant stream of activities kept taking my time away ("distracting me") from doing the work of my business (then consulting services)! The harder I tried to get rid of those tasks, the more there were. Can you relate? As I began working with a mentor, taking classes, and otherwise learning more about marketing – as you are doing now – I learned three important lessons:

Marketing Lesson Number 1: Marketing is critical to your success.

Here's why: without marketing, you will not have clients;
Without clients, you will not have revenues;
Without revenues, your business will not succeed (unless, of course, you want to offer your service for free and do not need it to generate income for you to consider it a success!)

So I needed to learn what kinds of marketing were best for my business and how to integrate those strategies into my business activities on a *regular basis* to succeed. Which leads directly to the next lesson.

Marketing Lesson Number 2: As a basic guideline, at least 20 percent of your time each week should be spent marketing.

That's one day out of every five, or four to five days per month (assuming 20-22 work days per month). During the first year of your business, this may be as high as 50 percent! Does this surprise you? It does many new coaches. This concept will make more sense as you learn more about what activities actually constitute marketing. It's so much more than just calling prospective clients, preparing the copy for your yellow pages advertisement, and designing your web site. These are primarily *direct* strategies, and as we will see later in this chapter, it is the *indirect* strategies that create the best results for most coaches and other professional service providers.

Now I can hear your mental wheels spinning: "Fifty percent of my time? And I'm not getting paid for this?? How am I supposed to build a business that way?" Read on for Lesson Number 3.

Marketing Lesson Number 3: While you don't bill for marketing directly, you can get paid for the time you spend marketing by using the GEMS Formula described in **Launch Your Practice,** *rather than doing it arbitrarily.*

Your marketing time is not "wasted" time – after all, as Lesson Number 1 tells us, it is critical to your business's very existence. In the first volume of this series, we gave you a formula for fee setting. Remember those days you allotted to marketing and practice development? That is how you get paid for your marketing time! So you can put that concern to rest while we establish some of the initial dimensions of your business.

Notes:

Becoming a Master Marketer

By now you understand that you must learn marketing to become successful. You had hoped you could hire someone to do that for you – but, in fact, you are the best person to market your services in most cases. After all, coaching involves a personal relationship with the client and requires a good personality "fit" to succeed (more on this in chapter 12). So let me challenge you to take this one step further. Can you see yourself not just as someone who does marketing because you have to, but as a Master Marketer? That is, someone who is highly skilled at communicating to others what they do so that it is irresistible to them?

You know at least one person like this already. Think about someone you admire, whether in your current circle of acquaintances or someone famous. Master Marketers in the media might include Tony Robbins, Brian Tracy, Tommy Hopkins (the sales training guru), and others. Or it may be a consultant well known for his/her work training others in sales and marketing such as Jay Abraham, Doug Hall (author of *Jump Start Your Business Brain*) and others.

Think about someone you see as a Master Marketer. What are their characteristics? In the space below, list the things that set these people apart:

Here are some traits listed by students in our classes that characterize Master Marketers:

- Great storytellers
- Create perceived value – whether they actually have it or not
- Innovators – do things in a new way
- Meeting people where they are, speaking their language
- Connect emotionally

- Creating need
- Repetition, visibility
- Consistency
- Professional
- Persistent
- Extremely creative
- Focused
- High energy
- Abundance mentality (giving person)
- Creating value, not just selling stuff
- Optimistic, positive
- Superb listening skills
- Who-based, not what-based
- Emotional connection
- Huge contact list
- Able to read people and customize style to fit the prospect
- Passionate

Now, please consider these questions:

How many of the traits listed above do you currently possess? Put a checkmark next to the ones you have.

Do you have other traits that will help you effectively reach your customers? List them below.

What are your options regarding the traits listed above that you do not presently have? Can you (a) partner with someone that has these characteristics or skills? (b) take classes to learn the skills you need? (c) shift your business focus so that the passion about your service/product naturally flows from within you? (d) other? Write your thoughts below or, if you prefer, note the appropriate letter (a-d) next to each trait above.

Remember: the more you know about marketing, the more powerful you become in growing your business to the level you desire. Marketing truly makes the difference between success and failure, struggle and ease, for today's coaches, consultants, and other infopreneurs.

Please complete Exercise 1 in the GEMS System Workbook before continuing to the next chapter.

2 | 2: The GEMS™ Approach to Marketing

Now that you know the importance of marketing, let's look at a system that, if followed, will help you get outstanding results.

If you were going to build a marketing system that was highly effective in building your business, what features would it need to have? What would it need to do? List those features below.

Here are a few attributes we believe are critical to your marketing system – and which we have built into the GEMS [our acronym for Generating and Executing a Marketing System – that Works!] system – along with the result each creates.

Your marketing system should:

	Activity	Result
1.	Position you as a one-of-a-kind brand – providing a unique service designed for one or more specific market segments	Virtually eliminates competition
2.	Operate 24 hours a day with minimal hands-on effort once implemented	Technology serves you, not the other way around
3.	Generate an ongoing supply of	Customers/clients

	qualified leads through a variety of channels	come to you (and you spend less time marketing and selling!)
4.	Result in a high rate of conversion (prospects becoming customers or clients, clients becoming repeat consumers) as it moves prospects and existing clients up the Ladder of Trust (discussed in volume 3 of this series)	Increases revenue per client – and per marketing initiative – over time
5.	Encourage feedback and gather data from customers to contribute to future product enhancement/development	You keep your finger on the "pulse" of your market with minimal effort
6.	Enable deep penetration within all aspects of each target market via multiple media and multiple points of entry, whether individuals or organizations	You are seen as the #1 expert in your field and industry – so clients respect you and seek you out
7.	Constantly be adding new contacts (via opt-in methods) to company database	Creates ever-increasing prospect pool for existing as well as new products and services
8.	Be systematized so that growth and increased volume can be managed with ease, yet personalized so that the lifetime value of each client is recognized	Balances scalability with personalization
9.	Leverage the Internet, email, smart autoresponders, FAQ, and other methods of technology to minimize need for hands-on "synchronous" activity	Frees your time to be spent as desired
10.	Result in a decreasing need for synchronous marketing time	Makes possible a 90% referral-based practice within one to two years

The GEMS™ System, diagrammed on the following page, is designed to meet each of these goals. You will work through each element of the system in the following chapters.

THE GEMS™ APPROACH TO MARKETING

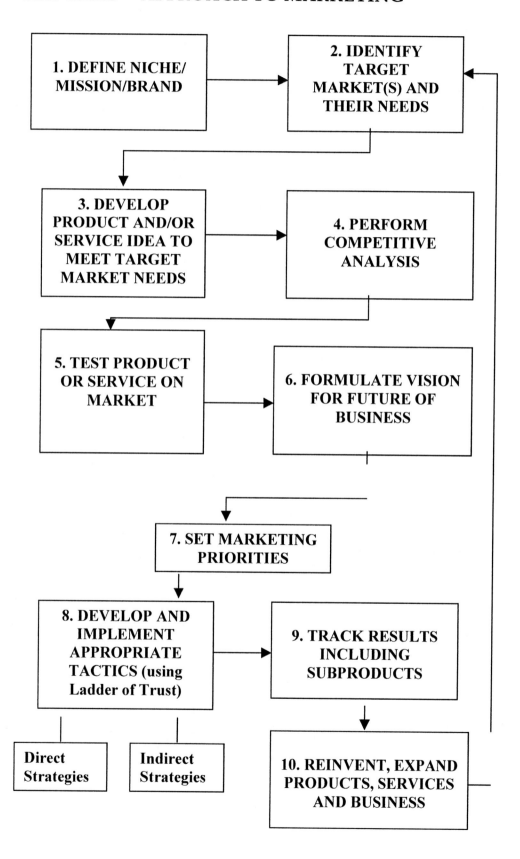

The GEMS process begins by defining your brand, which includes your business mission, your niche, and your business name. What identity will your business have? How will it be different from other businesses of similar type? (Note: businesses of "similar type" will be more than just other coaches in most cases! See chapter 7.)

Step 2 is to define up to three target groups, or markets, that the business will serve. This can be done by industry, age, location, demographic traits, size (if working with organizations), or any other common, identifiable traits. For each, you will need to determine their "hot buttons," or strong and immediate needs.

Step 3 will be to develop a draft list of one or more products and/or services that will satisfy these needs of your target market(s).

Step 4 involves evaluating your company – or prospective firm – in comparison to three types of competitors your prospects may also be considering. You will then learn how to distinguish yourself through further branding, virtually eliminating your competition.

Step 5 - Next, before spending a lot of money on fancy brochures, product prototypes, or other expensive business tools, you will do some low- or no-cost market testing to be sure your product/service ideas will be well-received within your target markets.

Step 6 - Now it's time to pull back (figuratively, at least), take a look forward 6 months, one year, 5 years, or more, and in Step 6 formulate a compelling, multi-sensory vision of your practice as you'd like it to develop.

Step 7 asks you to set some priorities in time, money, and other resources among the various tasks that lie ahead, and in Step 8 you finally begin to implement some tactics, both direct and indirect.

You continue on in Step 9 by tracking both the results of each campaign and the consistency (or lack thereof!) with which you perform the actions that you have found will lead to the results you want.

Then, in Step 10, you re-evaluate your product/service mix, analyze customer feedback and sales records, and begin to either refine existing products or develop new products and services – which takes you back through the steps once again.

Note to the Reader: You may notice that the work you are doing in this volume involves a lot of planning, thinking – even soul-searching! – and you will find yourself getting impatient to develop your web site, present a seminar, write an article, or implement other tactical strategies which we cover in *Fill Your Practice*. Why do we insist on this thinking process first? Because we want you to (a) succeed (!) and to (b) avoid losing or wasting money before you know exactly what you're doing! Many new coaching practices and other infopreneurships fail because of lack of planning. Yours will avoid that trap if you give thoughtful attention to the remaining chapters in this book before beginning the tactics part of your marketing process!

Please complete Exercise 2 in the GEMS System Workbook before continuing to the next chapter.

3

3: Dollars and Your Database

The GEMS™ system is a highly effective system for marketing coaching services – and for generating revenues. It has been proven by numerous coaches, consultants, and other infopreneurs for nearly two decades. But will it work for you? It will – *unless* you are holding onto limiting beliefs about money.

Examining Your Beliefs About Money

What do our beliefs about money have to do with marketing? Plenty! If you are seeking water and you go to the seashore with a thimble in your hand, you can certainly fill the thimble and say your container is full. But you could also bring a bucket, a bathtub – or even build a pipeline directly from the ocean to your town! In every case, the water would fill the size of container presented – but if you only fill a thimble or a bucket, you are missing out on much more that is readily available if you bring a larger container with you. Correspondingly, if childhood beliefs about money lead you to believe that you are only "worth" enough to get by, that it is only okay to earn x amount of money, or that it is only acceptable for other people (not you) to become financially independent, your beliefs will define – and may limit – your reality.

1. Think back to your childhood. What were you taught about money by your parents and other influential people? Write them here.

Perhaps you can relate to some of these ideas, which other coaches have related they were taught during childhood:

- Money doesn't grow on trees
- Money is vanity, so don't talk about it
- You should be afraid if you don't have enough money
- Money is hard to get, so maybe you shouldn't try
- The rich are evil, snobbish people
- Money is the root of all evil
- Save your money; there may not be more where that came from
- Money only comes to those who work hard

2. Now, taking each of the beliefs you were taught, what other beliefs have you developed to support those beliefs? For example, "Money doesn't grow on trees" might be supported by beliefs like "I need to hoard everything I make," "Never invest in aggressive growth investments," etc. Write them below, using the format given.

Core belief

Support belief   Support belief

Regardless of what each of us was taught as a child, we have the opportunity to re-examine those beliefs and messages as adults and decide whether we wish them to be part of our adult belief system. For each of the beliefs you identified in list 1 above, put an "A" next to those you accept and embrace as part of your current belief system, and an "R" for those you reject.

Wouldn't it be nice if it were as easy as that? That just by marking "R" next to something to indicate we reject it, it was gone? For most of us, however, those early messages (usually reinforced time and time again – maybe to this date if our parents are still alive) do not go away easily. Here are some tips for transforming your beliefs about money:

Transforming Your Beliefs

1. Identify the old belief – the belief you wish to transform.
2. Write out a description of the negative consequences this belief has caused you. (e.g., in the example above hoarding your money may have caused strife with your partner and/or kept you from feeling comfortable spending money that is needed for household necessities.)
3. Write the new belief with which you want to replace the old one. State it in the present tense, positively, e.g., "I now choose a balance between saving and spending." Also include any new supporting beliefs you wish to embrace.
4. Write out the ways in which you think this new belief will have positive results in your life.
5. State your new belief out loud, often throughout each day. Write it on index cards or sticky notes and put them where you will see them frequently. Reinforce this new belief for at least 21 consecutive days.
6. Keep a prosperity journal, identifying *specific* evidence that the new belief is creating positive results in your life. (This will keep you looking for the experience you want, which will in turn tend to make it a self-fulfilling prophecy.)

For more principles of prosperity to help you transform self-defeating beliefs about money, we recommend *Spiritual Economics* by Eric Butterworth.

Your Database

As a coach working in an information-based economy, perhaps your most valuable asset is your database. By *database*, we mean *customers or clients with whom you have done business, as well as prospects who have indicated some level of interest in your services.*   The faster your database grows, the more people you have available to promote existing and new products and services. Another benefit: you also have more prospects for the products and services of others from whom you may earn referral fees, commissions, or payments under an affiliate program (all discussed in *Fill Your Practice* in this series).

Consider the value of just one new client. Is it worth the amount he/she pays you for the service currently being provided, or more?

Lifetime value of client:

$300/month x 6 months coaching now = $1800

10 career transitions in life x $1800 = $18,000

Number of lifetime referrals: 5 x $18,000 = $90,000

Total value of this client = $18,000 + $90,000 = **$108,000 MINIMUM** (excluding other services and products you develop which client may purchase in the future)

Does this change the way you treat a prospect call? How? Write a few specific things you will do differently with this awareness in mind:

As you complete the steps in the GEMS™ system, you will begin to develop some products and services you want to promote. To prepare you for that step, I am going to ask you to begin aggregating your database *now* if you are not already doing so. It's never too soon – or too late! – to start! See Exercise 3.

Please complete Exercise 3 in the GEMS System Workbook before continuing to the next chapter.

4: Brand You – Your Unique Business Identity

The single most common mistake I have observed new coaches and other infopreneurs make is trying to be all things to all people. They feel pressure to make money, so they take any business that comes in the door (whether a physical door or a virtual one!). They hesitate to narrow themselves to a specific industry or demographic market for fear they will exclude too many customers. In chapter 5, you will analyze your proposed target markets for financial viability; that is another issue. But at this juncture, let me urge you to avoid making this mistake. Branding, niche-ing, and/or claiming your unique market space is the key to building a practice quickly that is both profitable and self-perpetuating.

The elements of defining your brand are (a) business mission, (b) business name and, if different, domain name (if different), and (c) Unique Value Proposition or UVP.

The Importance of Branding

If you were planning a romantic weekend and could choose between the following options, which would you choose?

> *Product 1:* a night at Chain Hotel A with generic room furnishings and no meals included
>
> *Product 2:* a Honeymoon Package at a lakeside bed and breakfast called "Romantic Getaway Lodge" which included a homemade breakfast and a bottle of champagne

Put another way: would you prefer to create a business that uniquely melds your talents with a need strongly felt by a group of people in the market, or one that is just like dozens of others?

Hopefully, these two examples, taken from both the customer's and the provider's perspective, illustrate the importance of branding. People are too overwhelmed with information today to sort through generic offerings and find one that will work for them. Given a choice, they will choose the targeted, customized, "branded" option that has been designed with their particular needs in mind.

Your *brand*, quite simply, is *the essence of what you offer stated in a highly marketable way that generates interest within people in your target market(s).* It combines your natural and learned talents with appropriate "packaging" (yes, even services can be packaged!) and offers them to people for whom they can be beneficial.

As Tom Peters aptly predicts, "It's Brand YOU or canned you; become distinct or extinct." Your brand causes you to become well known and actually evolves into the way you connect – meaningfully – with those you serve.

What elements do you already know will be part of your brand? Jot your thoughts here:

Your Business Mission

One of the foundational elements of your brand is the mission to which your business is dedicated. You must be sure you are clear as to what product or service you are selling, and to whom. You should then be able to tell others, in one simple sentence, what your business mission (or purpose) is. Your mission statement should answer these questions:

- What is the essence of your business?
- What values does it stand for?
- How would you describe the philosophy of your business?
- How is what you offer different (or better) than your competition?
- What customer need are you satisfying that is not currently being met?
- How does your business mission express your life purpose?

If you have completed CCI's Authentic Vocation™ Worksheet 1, Life Purpose, you know your answers to the 10 Clues to Your Life Purpose, have listed the themes your answers present, and have articulated a two-part life purpose statement. (And just in case you haven't, it is reprinted in exercise 4a for your use.) It should be stated in this way:

"My life purpose is to [insert the *essence,* or unchanging part of your purpose here, as in "help reduce discord among people"] through [here, insert the *expression* portion, which reflects the environment and scenarios through which you express your purpose at this point in your life; it will change as time goes on]."

This purpose then becomes the organizing principle of your life – including your business. Each time you are faced with a decision as to whether to accept a new client, whether to take a job, whether to build a relationship with someone, or whether to explore a new hobby, you use your life purpose as the filter. Does that person, activity, or option enhance your expression of your life purpose or detract from it? In your business, you use your life purpose and mission to decide what products and services to develop and offer, as well as whether or not to accept a particular client or project. If it enhances the expression of your life purpose, it is a good option for you to pursue (everything else being equal).

As an infopreneur, your business mission should in turn express your life purpose. Here's an example:

Life purpose: My life purpose is to help people (including myself!) realize and express their potential. I do this through my work as a coach, proactive parenting, volunteering with Outward Bound, my books, CD's and other products, and sharing with groups through speaking tools they can use to tap into their own potential.

Business mission: My business, Increase Your Potential, is dedicated to helping both under-performers and high performers realize and express more of their potential. Its services include coaching, information products, interactive web self-assessments, training programs, and speaking services for individuals in the food services industry.

Please complete Exercise 4b, My Company Mission Statement, in the GEMS Workbook now. Once you have drafted your mission statement, ask yourself whether the mission you have stated is consistent with your overall life purpose in exercise 4a. Your target markets and product mix (to be developed in future chapters) can also be subjected to this "acid test" to help you make choices that will increase your fulfillment while building your revenues.

Notes:

Naming Your Business

Choosing Your Business Name

Your business name can be selected before or after you outline your business mission. For some people, knowing the key values and aspects of the business as expressed in the mission statement helps them decide on a name. Others find it hard to articulate a mission without a name to work from. Please do this in the way that works best for you.

Your business name is usually identical to your domain name on the Internet (sometimes leaving out the suffix such as .com or .biz). In fact, it is usually more difficult to find an available domain name than it is to find a name that is "available" for use in your state! This is because thousands of new web sites are launched every day on the Internet, and many common descriptive domain names are already in use.

To check for availability, it is not enough to simply type the proposed domain name into your favorite browser and see if a web site appears. You must go to the domain name registry at www.networksolutions.com or www.register.com and inquire there for availability. If the name is reserved but a web site has not yet been built using it, you will nonetheless be prohibited from using it. (If it's a name you really like and it's not currently in use, you may consider printing out the contact information for the current owner from the registry site above and call, write or email them to see if they would be willing to sell or assign the domain name to you.)

We do *not* recommend registering the .net, .biz or .us version of a .com URL that is already in use; for example, if you wanted to call your business www.increaseyourpotential.com and someone already has that name in use for his business, but www.increaseyourpotential.net is available. The reason we recommend against your registering this .net name is because you may unintentionally help the .com business brand! And people have a tendency to forget the suffix for a domain name. If they went to the .com site by mistake – and liked what they saw! (particularly if it was a directly competing business) – you may lose a customer! At a minimum, it increases the number of hits to the .com site and effectively "brands" someone else's name – not yours! Don't help someone else brand – claim your own market space!

There are four types of business names that you could use:

1. your name, coach [or other professional title]
2. descriptive name of services ("Value Added Coaching")

3. combination ("Jane's Career Coaching")
4. abstract (e.g., Kodak) – generally not recommended for consulting or coaching because it takes too long to build name recognition

In choosing your business name, consider how you want to be remembered by your clients. A long domain name is not necessarily a negative *if* it is easy to remember. It can in fact be easier for clients to use and remember than a series of initials in a "cute" acronym that can easily be mixed up.

We also recommend that once you have narrowed it down to two or three "finalists," you submit them to several colleagues or friends and ask their first impression of the names. What does the name bring to mind? (It might have another meaning or nuance that you didn't intend!) Which has the most appeal for the type of business you are forming? If you decide to have a logo designed for your business, you can use the same process to bring a broader perspective than yours alone to the final choice of this important "image" for your business.

So how are you doing with your business name? Are you coming up with some ideas, or still feeling stuck? It is, of course, an important decision what you decide to call your business. And it is not unusual for new coaches and other infopreneurs to spend several weeks developing ideas, checking to find that many of their first choices are unavailable as domain names, developing more ideas, and having trouble deciding which is best. That's normal; don't be discouraged! Here's another exercise that can help you break out of "analysis paralysis" regarding your business name:

The Puzzle of Your Business Name

Write down, in brainstorming fashion, a list of words you would like to consider for inclusion in your business name; values that are important in your business; your life purpose statement; one- or two-word product or service descriptions; and any other words that describe an aspect of your desired business. You may wish to use a thesaurus to generate other possibilities for each as well.

Then, get a set of 3 x 5 note cards and write each of these words on individual cards. Spread them out on a table or on the floor. Now, pretend they are pieces of a jigsaw puzzle. Your business name is in there somewhere! Keep re-arranging the cards, setting off to the side those you wish to eliminate, and see what unique business names you can create from those words.

List your choices on a piece of paper; check for availability; then gather your colleagues' input and make your choice.

My chosen business name is: _____

Registering your business name

Registering your business name involves both domain name registration and registration with your state authority.

1. *Domain Name Registration.* Once you find a domain name that is available (see previous section), you can then register it. While you can register your name at www.networksolutions.com, it is more expensive than other discounted domain registration sites such as www.aitdomains.com, http://hosting.verio.com, http://registrar.godaddy.com and others. Typical discounted fees for registration are from $8 to $20 per year. We suggest you register the domain only for one year to begin with, since it is possible you may change your business name during that first year. With most sites, you can "park" the domain at that site's server until you are ready to have your own web site launched. But once you find a name you like that's available, don't wait to register! Many infopreneurs find that while their chosen name was available one day, they paused to think further about and possibly come up with another name, and by the time they returned it had been reserved by someone else.

Be sure to keep your contact information with the domain name registrar current if you change addresses, email providers/addresses, or phone numbers. You do not want your registration to lapse and risk someone else buying your name and building their own business with it after all of your hard work!

2. *Registration with your state.* The only criteria a business name must satisfy in most U.S. states is that it be at least one word different from all other business names on file within the county or counties in which you wish to register. The requirements generally are that you must register your business name only in the county and state in which your business is based, not in every location where you will do business.

To determine the registration procedures in your state, call your state's Corporation Division or Business Name Registry (both often found within the Secretary of State's office in the capitol city of your state) to ascertain whether the name you have chosen can be used and what is required for registration. If the name is available, you must register it before doing business under it. Failure to register your business name can subject you to fines and other penalties.

Of the four types of business names listed previously, the first of the four (your name only) does not require registration with most states, since you are using only your name. For each of the other three, you will need to file an Assumed Business Name Registration or Fictitious Name Registration form. If you have decided (using the information provided in *Launch Your Business* in this series) to form a corporation, partnership, or limited liability company, your business name filing is deemed completed when you file your Articles of Incorporation or Articles of Organization; no separate registration is needed in most states.

Notes:

Your Unique Value Proposition (UVP)

The final aspect of your brand is your UVP: what is different about what you offer from others in your field? Note that your list of services (e.g., financial consultant or career coach) is different from your UVP (e.g., assisting clients obtain maximum return on their investments). For most coaches and other infopreneurs, it takes some practice to learn to think and talk/write in terms of benefits instead of features. Remember:

> services = *features* of your business, titles, credentials, past history
>
> UVP = key *benefit(s)* offered to clients (from their perspective)

Here are a few examples:

Feature	Benefits
estate planning	peace of mind, financial security
career coaching	clarity (vs. confusion), fulfillment, financial resource to provide income
tax return preparation	eliminates fear of noncompliance, can result in getting refund (income) faster
computer training program	increased income, more challenging work, greater ability to support family

Are you starting to understand the difference? Please complete the two following sentences. (We'll develop your products and services more in the coming chapters.)

Primary services my business will (or does) provide: _____

_____

The key benefit I offer my clients through these services is: _____

_____

Are you still unsure how you stand out? Or what is (or can be) different about your business versus other similar professionals? It is often helpful to look at four key components in formulating your UVP:

- Strengths (assets you bring to the business and your markets),
- Weaknesses (things you don't do well and/or would like to delegate),
- Opportunities (micro- or macro-trends in the marketplace and specifically the target markets you will be serving that you can satisfy), and
- Threats (competitive pressures, lack of start-up capital, or any other external factors that could make it difficult for you to begin or expand your business)

The SWOT Analysis in Exercise 4c will help you clarify your UVP.

Please complete Exercise 4 in the GEMS System Workbook before continuing to the next chapter.

5: Your Target Markets

Now that you have begun to define your business mission, name, and brand, you will need to consider the kinds of people (or businesses) that will want to purchase your products or services. Then, and only then, you can design your marketing efforts to attract those people, rather than wasting dollars and time on an unproductive "shotgun" approach (i.e., trying to sell to "everyone" or to "anyone who will buy").

Defining Your Target Market(s)

You will want to describe the prospective customers in your target market first by their demographic characteristics. For individual clients, these might include sex, age, family status, and any other traits or situational characteristics. For business clients, you will want to designate industry, location (if relevant), size, gross income, and the title of the person in the company you will be seeking to reach. Exercise 5 will assist you with this.

How Many Target Markets to Have

If, as a new coach, you have managed to avoid the error of the shotgun approach, you must also take care to avoid another trap: relying too much on one client or market.

What are the dangers of relying on one major client (no matter how good the work!)? Write your answers here:

The primary danger is this: you put your entire business at risk by relying too much on one client – or one target market. If that business disappears or that industry takes a downturn (as the information technology business did in 2000), you are forced to virtually start from scratch in developing a new market.

The best coaches (as well as other infopreneurs, consultants, and business people) build their target markets strategically and deliberately, beginning with one and, once they achieve some penetration in that market, begin a second, and then a third. No fewer and no more than 3 is the ideal number. Why? See the following diagram, which illustrates cash flow cycles of each of three target markets:

The primary benefit? Your income smoothes out, following the average or midline of the three target markets (the dotted line in the diagram above) – and you avoid the "roller coaster effect" of extreme highs and lows of income that is experienced by many new coaches who have only one target market or client.

To begin, list below 3-5 target markets with which you would like to consider working..   Remember, they can be defined by any traits, character, or life/business situations they have in common – e.g., age, industry, gender, a common experience such as job loss or dissatisfaction with work, etc.

Target Market 1: _____
_____

Target Market 2: _____
_____

Target Market 3: _____
_____

Target Market 4: _____
_____

Target Market 5: _____
_____

Then, ask the questions in the next section about each of these target markets to narrow your list to 3 and to begin to set priorities as to which one will be the first you approach.

* * * * * * * * * * * * * * * *

QUESTIONS TO ASK ABOUT YOUR TARGET MARKET

by Paul Lemberg

1. Who is the target market? (You'd be surprised how many people don't have clear answers to this one.)
2. Do you "like" your market - do you feel comfortable in it? Are these the people you are inspired by doing business with?
3. Do the people in this market spend money on solutions like yours? And is it enough money?
4. How many individual buyers are there? (Companies or individuals.)
5. Is this number growing or shrinking?
6. What is the total sales volume of the market? (How much product or service do the prospective customers sell, in total?)
7. Is this number growing or shrinking?
8. Are the buyer's businesses more or less profitable than previously?
9. What are the key trends in the market?
10. What problems does your offering solve? Are these still interesting problems, current problems for market participants?
11. What is the value of solving those problems, in hard dollar terms?
12. What can your buyers afford to spend on your product or service?
13. What is the price range for other competitive products/services?
14. What is typical transaction size, and how often do they occur per customer?
15. Who are the key competitors?
16. How are they doing? Is their business up or down?
17. How do they get their new customers?
18. What are the key themes in the market lately?
19. What are people talking about? What are they writing about?
20. What print media target the buyers?
21. What web sites are dedicated to the buyers?
22. What associations does the market belong to?
23. Do people in the market talk to each other - is there strong word of mouth?
24. Who are the opinion makers in the market?
25. Can you influence these people?

Paul Lemberg is the author of *Faster Than the Speed of Change*, available at http://www.lemberg.com/faster.html or your local bookseller. (Send an email mailto:bookexrp@lemberg.com for a brief excerpt.) Copyright © Paul Lemberg; reprinted with permission.

"Hot Buttons"

Questions 10-19 in Paul Lemberg's list above inquire into the key needs or "hot buttons" of the target market. For your business to succeed, you must understand your customers' needs intimately. In addition to the questions presented, you can use these strategies to discover their "hot buttons":

- Read the leading trade journals in the industry; what are the themes you notice? Is there recent legislation with which they need to deal?
- Look for the basic human needs of money, love, and power; how are they expressed or relevant to your market(s)?
- Do an informal survey of people within your target market group
- Talk to the president of a trade association which serves that group
- Get your competitors' marketing materials and analyze what needs they purport to meet – these are clues to the clients' hot buttons

Based on your analysis so far, have you narrowed your list of target markets? Do you know which one to approach first? List them in order here:

Market 1: _____

Market 2: _____

Market 3: _____

As a general rule, you should be able to achieve some penetration within market number 1 within 6-9 months of launching your business. You can then begin working with market number 2 and, 6-9 months later or so, market number 3. So within 2 years you should have clients in all 3 markets and have some name recognition as an expert in those markets. Remember, we will discuss the tactics for doing this in the next volume, *Fill Your Practice*.

If you are still having difficulty determining which markets are best for you, consider the following suggestions from Christopher Lisle. Nothing is forever so don't belabor this choice process too much! You can always change your target later if it seems advisable to do so. And indeed, simply observing what kinds of clients do respond favorably to your services will help you further clarify your targets – and perhaps even enter markets you hadn't planned to!

"Considerations for Market Entry"
By Christopher "Kit" Lisle

Assessing the attractiveness of a market need not be difficult or time-consuming. It does require some research, and some thought, but the process should not be intimidating. The following article should serve as a brief guide for strategic planners considering the prospect of entering unfamiliar markets.

Rather than remaining opportunistic and open-minded about any market, develop a "short list" of markets of interest.
"If a man knows not what harbor he seeks, any wind is the right wind." Companies contemplating expansion into new markets should first create a list of markets or segments for consideration. Some strategic planners argue that "We are opportunistic and do not want to rule anything out. We will recognize the right market when we see it." As a result, these planners spend much of their time evaluating acquisition "opportunities" in industries that they later learn are unworthy of investment. That reactive method is often a waste of time. It is much more effective first to develop an understanding of "attractive" markets worthy of consideration for entry, then assess the "opportunities" within those target markets.

Determine if your firm has a clear advantage over other prospective entrants or existing players.
Because of your unique technology, experience, and access to customers, your firm could overcome some of the barriers to entry that may appear imposing to other prospective new entrants. An ideal market for entry is one in which your firm has a clear advantage over other prospective entrants or even the existing competitors.

Identify an unmet market need or underserved market niche.
Your firm may have discovered an underserved market niche. While other competitors are either not aware of a particular customer need, or are unable to serve it, you may have the unique ability to please customers. Market entry makes a lot of sense when your firm has discovered an unmet market need or an underserved niche.

Find the "Goldilocks" sized market.
The ability to influence or have a strong impact on the industry is hardly enough reason to justify entry; the potential new entrant must take the size of the market opportunity into account. While many strategic planners look for the obscure, niche segment and shy away from markets large enough to accommodate the proverbial "800 pound gorilla," most would agree that the smaller the market,

the more difficult it is to justify entry. Your best bet may be a "Goldilocks" market – neither too large, nor too small.

Look for a growing pie so that your slice does not have to come from other players.
An adequately sized, but shrinking market, is obviously less attractive than one that is rapidly growing. The growth rate of the market should be considered prior to making a decision about market entry. It is much easier to enter a growing market than it is to enter a market by stealing share from other players.

Conduct your own Competitive Analysis of each market under consideration.
Michael Porter, a long-time Harvard Business School professor and author of *Competitive Advantage* and *Competitive Strategy*, established a simple framework to assess the attractiveness of a market. For Porter, the level of competition in the industry is a very important factor. He segments his analysis of competition into Five Forces that shape the industry: The Bargaining Power of Customers; The Bargaining Power of Suppliers; The Threat of Substitute Products; The Threat of New Entrants; and the Current State of Rivalry Among Existing Competitors in the Industry.

A perfect market would serve customers who are small, powerless, and highly dependent upon the industry's competitors. There would be a large number of relatively similar suppliers to the industry in question, each of whom places great value on the business of its customers. The Bargaining Power of Suppliers and of Customers would therefore be low. The industry would be innovative and would involve substantial barriers to entry so that the Threats of Substitute Products and New Entrants would also be low. Finally, there would be enough competitors and enough price elasticity so that the level of Internal Rivalry Among Existing Competitors would not be high.

Identify markets that are in a state of "disequilibrium."
Porter would also look for a market that is undergoing some degree of change or transformation ("disequilibrium"). A stagnant industry is less likely to embrace a new entrant. An industry that is seeking new solutions, on the other hand, is much more of an opportunity.

Find pockets of unhappy customers with low switching costs.
Similarly, an industry whose customers are not being well served could easily accommodate an aggressive, customer-focused new entrant. The level of customer satisfaction in some industries is shamefully low. New entrants may wish to assess the level of customer satisfaction, their difficulty of switching suppliers, and the process that major customers go through in selecting a new supplier. You may also wish to consider your firm's unique differentiation and

how it may affect the industry's structure, reduce customer costs, or improve upon the industry's standards of product quality. If customers are generally happy, switching costs are high, and price is the most important purchase decision factor, you may want to look for another market.

It may seem obvious, but...all else being equal, choose the more profitable of two markets.

If you can choose your market (and that is what this article is trying to convince you to do), you might as well choose one that is profitable. One could argue that the stakes are higher in profitable markets. One could also argue that large players are attracted to profitable markets. I agree. But if you find two markets that are attractive to you based upon the previously mentioned factors, I suggest that you identify and enter the more profitable one.

Observe macro-level trends.

If you still need to find a reason to justify market entry, consider the macro-level themes and trends that could impact the market. Does the aging of the baby-boomer population affect this industry in any way, for example? What about themes involving education reform, the environment, or the healthcare system? If so, the market could benefit and your entry could be made easier.

Identify the most attractive segment or segments.

Now that you have identified an attractive market, be as specific as possible. You will want to know which segments (in terms of product types, end-use customer types, and geography, for example) are most attractive. If you can identify the most attractive segments, you will have an excellent starting point for an acquisition search program – if you decide to enter the market via acquisition or joint venture.

Christopher "Kit" Lisle is the Managing Director of Acclaro Growth Partners, www.acclaropartners.com, a corporate growth advisor for middle-market companies and their sources of capital. Acclaro serves as a resource for companies wishing to receive value-added, actionable information and analysis about markets of interest. Lisle's email address is kitlisle@acclaropartners.com.

Please complete Exercise 5 in the GEMS Workbook before continuing to the next chapter.

6

6: Your Product Mix

By now you should have at least a tentative statement of your niche or brand – linking what's unique and special about you with the benefits you offer your clients. You should also have a list of one or more target markets (whether designated by demographic criteria, industry group, or a combination of both). But your marketing foundation is not yet complete! The next step in the GEMS™ System is to develop a range of products and services that will meet the needs of your target markets.

For many coaches, their coaching services are their core offering. But as we illustrated in the chapter on fee setting in *Launch Your Practice,* you only have so many hours in the day! And maybe you want to spend some of those hours doing something other than coaching, right? Creating products such as articles, books, CD's, interactive web-enabled programs (e.g. a self-assessment tool), e-books, and the like, allows you to increase your revenues without increasing the time you spend working each week. (We will discuss all of these and many more tactical options in *Fill Your Practice,* Volume 3 of this series.)

Here are two important principles to remember as you consider how to structure your product/service offerings:

Principle 1. Package your services. Bundling or packaging your services is both a way to increase your profits and customize your service to each individual client. Consider the following "Sample Coaching Packages," integrating CCI's 8-step Authentic Vocation™ process and QuantumShift!™ coaching techniques, for examples of how you might apply this in the career coaching context:

SAMPLE COACHING PACKAGES

Package 1: Discover Your Authentic Vocation™

This package is right for people who are in career transition or wish to find a more satisfying job. You receive support in both identifying the right job/career direction for you and developing and implementing a successful campaign to find it. Includes all elements of both the "Find Your Career Direction" package and the "Jump Start Your Job Search" packages.

You receive:
- 24 personalized coaching sessions (a $3000 value)
- Two assessments (chosen to fit your needs and goals) (a $200 value)
- 8 Authentic Vocation™ worksheets, each one to help you define a different aspect of your ideal job and career
- Two resumes written by our certified professional resume writer, Mary Writer (a $300 value)
- Excel spreadsheets on which to co-design, with your coach, the optimum approach to your job search and track your weekly activity
- 12 weeks of admission to our weekly [or biweekly] Job Search Networkers Group (a $120 value)
- A comprehensive workbook and a Resource Guide to guide your discovery process (a $50 value) [NOTE: CCI provides tools to use in this way]
- Email support between coaching sessions (up to 5 per week)

Investment: You receive a total of over $3700 worth of services for just $2995! Or include just 12 coaching sessions and package price is $1495. Additional discount available for prepayment; installment arrangements available and all credit cards accepted.

Package 2: Find Your Career Direction

This package is designed to help you redefine your job or career to achieve your changing goals and needs. We focus on identifying at least 3-5 viable job/career directions for you that meet all 8 criteria of the revolutionary Authentic Vocation™ method. Say goodbye to confusion – this program will help you find clarity!

You receive:
- 12 personalized coaching sessions (a $1500 value)
- One assessment (chosen to fit your needs and goals) (a $100 value)
- 8 Authentic Vocation™ worksheets, each one to help you define a different aspect of your ideal job and career
- A comprehensive workbook, *Discover Your Authentic Vocation*, to guide your discovery process (a $25 value)
- Email support between coaching sessions (up to 3 per week)

Investment: You receive a total of over $1650 worth of services for just $1295. Additional discount available for prepayment; installment arrangements available and all credit cards accepted.

Package 3: Jump Start Your Job Search!

This package is designed to help you redefine your job or career to achieve your changing goals and needs. We focus on identifying at least 3-5 viable job/career directions for you that meet all 8 criteria of the revolutionary Authentic Vocation™ method. Say goodbye to confusion – this program will help you find clarity!

You receive:

- 12 personalized coaching sessions (a $1500 value)
- One assessment (chosen to fit your needs and goals) (a $100 value)
- A comprehensive resource manual, *Turbo-Charge Your Job Search,* to guide your job search (a $25 value)
- Excel spreadsheets on which to co-design, with your coach, the optimum approach to your job search and track your weekly activity
- Two resumes written by our certified professional resume writer, Mary Writer (a $300 value)
- 12 weeks of admission to our weekly [or biweekly] Job Search Networkers Group (a $120 value)
- Email support between coaching sessions (up to 3 per week)

Investment: You receive a total of over $2100 worth of services for just $1695.

Optional Package 4: Coaching "a la carte"

If you are on a budget and want a "no-frills" approach to career discovery or job search, consider our "a la carte" package. You receive 12 personalized half-hour coaching sessions, valued at $1500, for $1295 under this program.

Principle 2. Give your prospects three choices. Marketing research tells us that given three choices, 67 percent of people will choose the second of the three. So instead of telling your clients "My coaching services cost $900 for 90 days, would you like to purchase them?" – which gives them only two choices, yes or no – offer them three levels of service (as in the example depicted above). Two-thirds of them will choose the second level of service and your revenues will increase with this strategy alone.

Please complete Exercise 6 in the GEMS Workbook before continuing to the next chapter.

7

7: Competitors and Perceived Competitors: How Do You Stack Up?

Knowing your competition, their products/services, their target markets, and how they bring those products/services to their customers will enable you to better define your own business niche and brand.

Your competition consists of three types of companies. Example: let's say you own a gourmet coffee shop and your market is the metropolitan area of your city.

    a.   **Direct competitors:** businesses with a similar mix of products and services to yours who are working with the same or different markets (example: other coffee shops)

    b.   **Overlapping competitors:** businesses offering **some** of the same types of products/services as you, but not all -- so there is an overlap with your business (example: stores that sell coffee, but don't serve it)

    c.   **Multidimensional competitors:** businesses offering what you offer -- and more (example: full-service restaurant or gourmet store OR a coffee shop with national market)

These three types of competitors are illustrated in the following diagram:

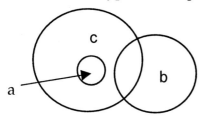

The way to determine whether or not a company is a competitor is to ask: "Would a person in my target market, or in the general public, view company x as being in the same or a similar business to mine?" If so, you must consider them among the service providers your customers may consider – even though, as we discussed in chapter 4, effective branding virtually eliminates competition by its nature.

What would be examples of the three types of competitors in coaching?

In career coaching, competitors may include other career coaches and career counselors ("a" competitors), resume writers and interview coaches ("b" competitors), and outplacement firms as well as possibly the One Stop Centers offered in every major city and state ("c" competitors).

In addition, you will need to compare your business, feature by feature, with your key competitors to see how you stack up – and how to distinguish your business from theirs.

Please complete Exercise 7 in the GEMS Workbook before continuing to the next chapter.

8 | 8: Market Testing That Gets You Business

By testing your product and service ideas on a small sampling of people before you finalize them, you can save tremendous time and money if something is not as well received as you had hoped. You can redesign, test again, and ultimately launch those offerings to which you know your clients will be receptive.

As with all other aspects of GEMS, we approach market testing from a strategic perspective. Rather than arbitrarily beginning to test a product or service that we think someone might want to buy, we need to first consider:

1. The characteristics of your target market (demographic and psychographic)
2. What products and services are already in the marketplace
3. What your competition is doing that may be perceived as competitive offerings
4. What price points are being used by others for similar products or services

Once we have examined these issues, we can consider which of the available techniques for market testing would be best for the product or service we are offering.

Techniques for Market Testing

There are a number of ways to do market testing. Thankfully it's much less expensive to test services than products, and the Internet has made it cheaper to test anything than it was in the pre-Internet era.

Some of the techniques you might use include:

- **Online surveys** (can use zoomerang.com or yahoogroups.com to manage the results)

Here's a sample survey used by a person wanting to start a business doing budgeting and bill paying:

1. Do you currently use an accountant? Yes/No

2. Do you have a written household budget? Yes/No

3. Does everyone in your household follow the budget plan? Yes/No

4. Who in the household is responsible for paying the bills? Husband/ Wife/ Outside service

5. How often are bills paid each month? Weekly/ By paycheck / Monthly

6. What percentage of your income do you currently put aside for savings? Less than 5 percent / 5 to 10 percent / More than 10 percent

7. How many times in the past five years were you in a financial bind due to unforeseen expenses? None / 1-5 / 5-10 / More than 10

8. How often in the past six months have you been late on any kind of payment? None / 1-6 / 6-12 / More than 12

9. How much time do you spend each week on your household finances? Less than 1 hour / 1-3 hours / More than 3 hours

10. How often do you reconcile your checkbook? Monthly / Quarterly / Whenever the mood strikes

What questions would you want to ask your target market about your services to both determine interest AND awaken them to the potential issues/needs they have for your services?   Write your ideas below.

- **Free sample program** (teleclass, coaching session, seminar, etc.) through a professional organization, local library, church, community education program, etc. You can then present your concepts and ask participants for their feedback, helping you develop a sort of "prototype" for the ultimate program, product or service you will offer.

Tips:

    ✓ Use a sponsor
    ✓ Do it on a very limited basis (so you aren't giving away too much)
    ✓ Give them information but leave them wanting for more!

Traps:

    ✓ Don't become known for giving your expertise away *too* much!
    ✓ Don't forget to get feedback from participants (evaluation form, verbal feedback, one-way mirror/focus group, etc.)

- **Ezine notice:** place a notice/blurb in one or more ezines about your proposed service or product

- **Informal in-person survey:** survey your existing database of clients to determine whether they would use this new service or product

- **Focus groups** (either standard formal process in which a group of people similarly situated to your target clients gather and answer a specified list of questions in group discussion fashion – or a more informal group discussion over coffee

- **Feedback and evaluation forms:** these should even be done with private coaching clients so you can continue to improve and determine other unsatisfied needs of your clients!

- **Newspaper inserts:** placing articles as inserts into newspapers where job fairs are advertised (and presentations at the job fairs to attendees)

- **R&D team:** Invite people you know (and perhaps those you don't through a notice on your web site or other means) to agree to provide input and feedback on a topic area or product idea over a stated length of time – e.g., 30 days. In exchange, they receive a gift (book, free mini-coaching session, tape or CD, etc.) for their time. I have also found that people enjoy tremendously seeing the responses of others to the same questions if, e.g., Yahoo groups or another online discussion list serve is used for the team. After the time is complete, you synthesize the information they have given you and finalize product offerings.

Please complete Exercise 8 in the GEMS Workbook before continuing to the next chapter.

9

9: Ten Most Common Marketing Mistakes -- and How to Avoid Them

Before moving on to your vision for your practice, let's re-visit what we've done so far. We have:

- Defined marketing
- Established a brand, mission, and business name
- Chosen three target markets to approach
- Assessed our positioning vis-à-vis our competition
- Begun to market test our service or product

Now, let's do something else successful people do: learn from others' mistakes! The following ten mistakes are frequently made by new coaches, consultants, writers, speakers and other infopreneurs. Review them now and be sure you don't fall prey to the same traps!

TEN TOP MARKETING MISTAKES SMALL BUSINESSES MAKE

© Roberta Gamza, JCTC, CEIP, CJST; reprinted with permission Career Ink, Louisville, CO rgamza@earthlink.net

So much to do, so little time!

The entrepreneur will always face the dilemma of time. That's why it's critical to have a business plan and a marketing plan to keep you focused on your goals and strategies so that you will achieve them. When you develop a strong marketing plan, and commit to it, it becomes clear where you should spend your marketing time and keeps you from getting sidetracked - wasting time on activities that have nothing to do with achieving your goals.

First of all, let's think about marketing. You do it every day. Every encounter and conversation you have with someone else is a marketing opportunity. Boiled down to its simplest form, marketing is leaving an impression. Every time you meet someone or interact with them you leave an impression behind. If it was a positive and memorable meeting, you remember the occasion. If it was meaningless, you forget about all the people you met and the activities that occurred.

You're already a master at marketing. You spruce yourself up before you leave the house. You are polite to the person in the grocery store. You hold the door for someone behind you or someone struggling with packages in their arms. You don't even think about these activities; they are natural to you. And they all leave an impression of some kind.

Marketing your business should come naturally to you once you demystify it and make it a manageable process. Effective marketing is not random; it is strategically planned and implemented. This article and the series of articles to follow will serve to demystify specific marketing concepts and activities. We begin with the 10 top marketing mistakes made by small businesses...

1. Thinking Small - Marketing is for Big Business, not me. Every business needs to market to attract customers and achieve its potential. Look at what big biz does and adapt it for your business. Be creative. You are not going to have the marketing or advertising budget of a large corporation, but you do have a budget, and when your marketing is successfully directed at your target audience, it will be effective. Define what the word "big" really means to you and your business. Maybe you want to employ 10 people. Maybe being a one-person shop earning $100,000+ a year is your idea of big. Whatever it is, stop thinking of yourself as being small. It can become a self-fulfilling prophecy. You must think big to grow big.

2. Thinking of marketing as an expense, when it is an investment. You can't afford not to market. Marketing is an investment with a big return. Your investment is time, money, and imagination. Marketing doesn't have to be expensive, just effective. Analyze each proposed activity, understand the investment, and forecast the result. Determine how much new business must be generated to return your initial investment. Can you recoup the investment in a reasonable amount of time? Once you've recouped the investment, will your marketing efforts continue to generate more sales? Would you get those sales if you did nothing? Only commit to those activities that give you a good return. Don't waste precious time on activities with a marginal return or that just break even. It's okay to pare down your original long list of marketing activities to just one, two, or three items. Once you know what will not work well for your business, you won't waste any precious time or money on the effort and won't be tempted by distractions.

3. Engaging in marketing activities only when business is down. To sustain a steady flow of business, marketing activities must be on-going and maintained. Marketing activities are rarely a one shot deal. They are sustained campaigns. Be patient. You won't see results overnight. Put a plan in place and give it time to work. If you abandon it too soon, you kill any chances of success it might have had. To top it off, you'll have to start all over, only this time you'll be even more impatient for having wasted time and money on the first plan.

Don't confuse marketing campaigns with sales incentives. Sales incentives are temporary price reductions or special services designed to generate short-term business. They are effective and should be used when business is down, but must be used sparingly. If sales incentives are your only activity used to generate new business, you are effectively devaluing your services and lowering your prices.

You should have sustained marketing activities that you do to keep your presence in front to prospective clients. These can include Yellow Pages advertisements, storefront presence, community sponsorships, targeted advertising, search engine registrations, and a whole list of other activities that are appropriate to your business goals. If you wait until business is slow before you market or launch sales incentive campaigns, it can be an uphill battle to get back on track.

4. Performing little or no market research. Know your competitors - the services they offer, their prices, the quality of their products and services, and how they differentiate themselves. To succeed you must be either competitive or unique. Knowing your competition does not mean you have to compete with them point for point, but you do need to address their offerings versus yours when a customer asks. This is how you will differentiate yourself. If you can be unique on many points, then you have an opportunity to control a market or niche. If you control a market or niche, you control pricing.

5. Failure to differentiate your business from your competition. You must differentiate your business from the competition, even if you are matching them point for point in services. Give clients a reason to select you rather than the others in your field. The most common ways to differentiate your business is by service offering, quality of customer service, credentials, experience, availability, or price. If all of these items are similar to those of your competition, then create another way to stand out. Do something the others don't, even it if means taking a risk. When customers call you shopping for services be sure your pitch includes your differentiators. Demonstrate your differentiation in your marketing or branding efforts (logo, business card, collateral, advertising, etc,) Remember the more unique you are, the more you control the market and market pricing.

6. Failure to segment and target the market. Even if your product/service is broad enough that everyone can benefit from it, not everyone is going to purchase it. Identify those most likely to purchase. Research further and know who in that market is the most profitable for you to work with. Key in on that audience and find out how to best reach them. Be sure you understand their needs and purchasing habits. See where they spend their time and money. Aim your marketing budget at those clients in the places they frequent.

7. Inadequate branding. The most valuable marketing tool you have is your business image (e.g., name, logo, tag line). Look around at big business. Their name/image is everywhere - paid advertising and sponsorships. It is never compromised. It always adheres to the corporate standards. You must do the same for your business and your brand. Never compromise your business image. Use it everywhere and make sure people remember it. Set a standard for its usage and stick with it. Have electronic files available for others to use so that your standards are constant. Put it on all your customer and presentation materials. Don't use standard PowerPoint presentation templates without modifying them with your logo. You're not advertising Microsoft; you're advertising your business.

8. Competing with the competition. Competing with the competition takes time, effort, and resources away from your core business. It is likely that there is more than enough business to sustain you and your competition. If you and the competition are very similar, you can work together and join forces to conquer the marketplace. If you are dissimilar, you can get to know each other's businesses and refer to each other. Identify the ways both businesses can become stronger by working together. There is power and synergy in partnering.

9. Thinking of sales, not profits! There are many activities that will generate sales, but will those sales be profitable? Sales incentives, temporary price reductions or special services designed to generate short-term business, are effective but should be used sparingly. They can eventually devalue your services. They definitely lower your prices and decrease your profit margins. You are in business to make a profit. Know what your profit margins are on each of your products/services. Sales to existing customers are far more profitable than sales to new customers. Keep this in mind when allocating your marketing budget.

10. Losing focus - expanding too early or unnecessarily. Know your core business and don't do anything to jeopardize that. When you consider expanding your product and service offerings, expanding into new markets or offering new services, thoroughly investigate the new and understand the impact it will have on the core business. Stay focused on your core business. Expansion is a double-edged sword. It can add bring incremental business and increase your profits, or it can dilute your core business, business identity, and revenue stream. Until you have worked out all the kinks in your core business, don't even consider expanding.

Marketing is an incredibly powerful tool. Poor marketing can kill an exceptional product and exceptional marketing can make a poor product remarkably successful. Powerful and effective marketing is the result of a solid, well thought-out plan, a little imagination, and creativity. Know who are you, where you are going, and how you are going to get there.

Please complete Exercise 9 in the GEMS Workbook before continuing to the next chapter.

10 10: Your Vision: What do You Want Your Practice to Be?

Now that you have defined your business name, mission, and niche, what do you want your business to "grow up" into? In this module, you will be developing a very vivid vision of what you want your business to be.

Simply defined, *vision* is *a vividly imagined picture of the future of your life or business, complete with emotions and all other senses incorporated into it.* Once you articulate your vision, you have something you can move "toward," a compelling force in the future that keeps you moving on.

As you state your vision, don't just say something like "I will be coaching people in making meaningful life changes." Rather, state it in the *present* tense ("I am") and describe how you feel, what you see, what you hear, what you taste, and any other sensory input that will be important as you make your dream real.
In the case of the marketing vision, you would be looking at how *your* marketing system would look, feel, taste, touch, act, be, do, etc. If you haven't written an overall vision, then it will probably be a mix of the overall and marketing; that will work as a starting point. But if you can put your ideal life on paper, it will begin to happen! There are several benefits of a written vision:

Benefits of a Written Vision Statement

1. *A written vision is automatically tested by your innate sense of what's possible.* If it seems crazy to you, the beliefs and action you have imagined supporting it will in fact not help you reach it – so you will need to find or identify others that do.

2. *A written vision provides you with clarity that will help you overcome resistance on the way to its manifestation.* This vision gives us the power and energy to look for a different way, to see how we need to change or transform, because it is worth it

3. *A written vision helps shed light on your passion and purpose as it relates to your business.* It is a necessary next step in making your ideal situation real.

4. *A written vision activates your emotions, in vivid color.* This is the time to use all the adjectives you learned in grade school: who, what, where, why...fulfilling, exciting, etc.

5. And most importantly, *a written vision is more likely to materialize!* Psychologists studied the Harvard graduating class of 1954 for a 20-year period.

They analyzed how many of the graduates had written goals and plans (which emerge from one's vision) at graduation, and 3 percent did. After 20 years, those 3 percent had a collective net worth that was greater than the *entire rest of the class!* And they also measured higher on questionnaires about life satisfaction and other subjective indicators of success. So your vision is worth doing!

Criteria for a Successful Vision

Your vision statement should satisfy at least five criteria in order to be most powerful. It should:

a) be written in the present tense
b) be open-ended,
c) be sufficiently specific so that you can recognize it when you see it – (it balances the two);
d) stretch your rational mind's beliefs about what is possible for you; and
e) focus on the feelings you will experience as the vision materializes.

[NOTE: There's a meta-strategy here! You can use this as a technique with your clients who are struggling to define their next steps too!]

Example:

> Upon graduating from the school of occupational therapy, I am employed in an autonomous position doing healing work 20 hours per week with children that honors the mind/body connection and including art therapy. I have my own practice with adults as well, spending 10 hours per week doing bodywork, music, counseling, and art therapy. I speak to groups regularly about the psycho-social-spiritual process.
>
> I make $50,000 or more per year from these activities. I feel energetic and fulfilled. I have time to enjoy life with my daughters, going camping, singing, and sharing meals together. I am enjoying and supporting my daughters through high school. I own my home, have a garden, and earn enough that I can hire help to clean the house and maintain the yard so I can enjoy my creative projects.

What else could be added to make this even more powerful?

How about: what the garden looks like, sounds of birds chirping, pace of work, description of the office, size and description of home, etc.

Please complete Exercise 10 in the GEMS Workbook before continuing to the next chapter.

11

11: Tapping Into the Law of Attraction

" Thought can attract to us that which we first mentally embody, that which has become a part of our mental makeup, a part of our inner understanding. Every person is surrounded by a thought atmosphere. This mental atmosphere is the direct result of his conscious and unconscious thought, which, in its turn, becomes the direct reason for, and cause of, that which comes into his life.   Through this power we are either attracting or repelling. Like attracts like and it is also true that we may become attracted to something which is greater than our previous experience, by first embodying the atmosphere of our desire."

-- Ernest Holmes, *The Science of Mind*

Another key principle in marketing and creating the kind of practice you want – which is operating in your experience whether you are conscious of it or not! – is the Law of Attraction. The above quote describes it well and includes the following 3 principles:

- *Everything that we now have in our life (and work!) was first a thought.* That's right: your clothing, your furniture, your car, your job, the people in your life – all began as a thought. So those fleeting ideas, fantasies, and daydreams that cross your mind during the day have the potential to become things – and so do the judgments, negative thoughts, and worries you entertain!

- *Thoughts, taken cumulatively, create a "thought atmosphere."* That thought atmosphere would, like a magnet, attract that which is like it ("positive charge") and repel that which is unlike it ("negative charge"). To change the things that are being attracted, one must change the charge. But what do we do instead? We manipulate the effects of that thought atmosphere. If negative, pessimistic people keep entering your life at work and spreading their negativity all around where you are, you might try to convince them they are wrong. You might try complaining. You might even say positive words. But if deep inside you have a pessimistic viewpoint yourself about the company's prospects, or believe that work is a "drag," you will unconsciously attract other people that reflect that thought atmosphere. So the best way to change the people and things in your life is to work on changing those inner beliefs – the *cause* that attracts those people and things – and when they change, the outer effects will change automatically.

- *If we want to experience something better than our current experience, we must first visualize it.* A vision is like a "seed" planted in the fertile soil of the greater Mind that begins to germinate. If we water and fertilize it by focusing on it, it will grow into a real, physical experience. For example, if we want more clients, more money, a nicer house, more supportive relationships, improved health, etc., we begin by clearly visualizing and thinking about that experience, or as the quote puts it "embodying the atmosphere of our desire." We use what we learned about vision in the last chapter to formulate a vivid description of our desired state. We focus on it daily, envisioning it as though it has occurred, and do our part to take the action that seems appropriate to lead to its happening.

How can these principles be applied in your practice?

A few ideas to get you started:

- If you don't have the income you want, the Law of Attraction says your thoughts are limiting the amount you believe you can have; to change, embody the atmosphere of greater wealth

- If you are attracting clients that don't have enough money to pay you, don't seem engaged in the process, or are otherwise different than your ideal profile, there is a part of you that is drawing that in! (Ouch!) Is there a part of you that needs to be resolved or healed in order to feel comfortable with higher functioning clients?

- If you see someone who is highly successful, making lots of money, good reputation, high quality clients, etc., they have first imagined it in their mind, combined it with strong emotions, and regularly focused on it while taking the necessary steps to make it real. And now you have attracted them into your experience (even if you're just reading about them!), so there is a part of you that is ready to have a similar experience in your own life. Follow their example!! Interview them if you can to find out exactly how they did it – you can avoid making the same mistakes by learning from their experience!

If there is any one thing that I have seen hold new coaches and infopreneurs back more than anything, it is *lack of confidence*. As we discussed in *Launch Your Practice* in the chapter on fee-setting, you are not a beginner! You bring all of your prior experience and training to the table – as well as your coach training if you have completed the Career Coach Institute or another program, and other continuing education and industry expertise. If you will simply complete the exercises in this book and use the principles outlined in chapter 10 on Vision to create a compelling future picture toward which to move, you will feel and convey to your prospects a sense of confidence. And that will translate to increased revenues, as it changes your thought atmosphere!

Please complete Exercise 11 in the GEMS Workbook before continuing to the next chapter.

12

12: When They Call, What Do You Say? Sales Strategies for Coaches

When you made the decision to explore – or begin – the business of coaching, your first unexpected discovery was that you would have to market yourself, right? We discussed that in chapter 1. But that wasn't the worst of it; you later found out that if you did your marketing well, you would also need to be the primary salesperson for your company. Most coaches and other infopreneurs react to that news as though they had just smelled a skunk in their back yard: yech!!

There is some good news: if you have built your marketing system so that most clients come to you (e.g., through a referral of a satisfied client with whom you have worked), the conversation isn't so much "selling" as discussing the client's needs and crafting a service package that will meet their needs. That's not so hard, is it? The following principles will help you take on this role with greater ease.

Principle 1: There's a big difference between knowing how to coach versus knowing how to market and sell your coaching services

Marketing and sales are not optional, but required, of the successful coach. The good news is, they can be learned! You must expand your skills to include selling as well as coaching. The coaches who have successful practices have mastered this added skill.

Principle 2: "Sales" is not a four-letter word.

Marketing is letting people know what you do; selling is telling a particular prospect what you can do to satisfy their needs. You must learn to translate the general to the specific in order to meet the needs of specific clients.

Principle 3: The master sales skill is knowing how to execute a professional intake session to determine what the prospect's needs are and how you can satisfy them.

You should have a standard list of questions that you ask a potential client in order to determine their needs and, as importantly, whether you can fulfill them.

Principle 4: Giving away your services is not in your best interest.

Other professionals don't give away their services for free; why should you as a coach? Subject yourself to the same standards as a doctor, lawyer or accountant, and get clients to pay for even their initial consultation with you! We will learn more in volume 3 about why offering free "trial" coaching sessions is a relatively ineffective and unprofitable strategy for most coaches.

Principle 5: If you don't know how to "sell" when you need to, you will leave some customers wanting.

Your job, when someone calls to inquire about your services, is to determine what their needs are (where they feel pain) and how you can meet it. Period. If all you can do is describe what you do in general terms, without relating it to the client's specific needs, you will miss out on some business that should be yours.

Coach as Salesperson

The following 10 principles will help you master the aspects of sales that you will need in your coaching practice.

1. Under promise, over deliver

Be sure not to promise more than you can deliver. [The ICF Standards of Ethical Conduct actually prohibit this – see item 3 below!] To test your offerings, have colleagues or friends read the descriptions of your proposed coaching services/packages and tell you objectively whether they sound reasonable as deliverables. Let the client be delighted when they get more than they expected! Knowing that customers will ideally be with us for life (remember chapter 3?), and that we want to build a referral-based practice, this becomes even more important.

2. Have at least three levels of service to offer, with respective fee levels

This is a practice from our "bible" of fee setting that says if people are offered three packages, 67 percent of them will choose the second level – and without the three levels to choose from, they'll spend less with you than they would in any event!

3. Clearly state what coaching is, and isn't

This is the place to define coaching, simply, and to clarify how it's different from therapy and from consulting; then as you introduce the coaching agreement you can elaborate further on these distinctions as you flesh out the roles of both coach and client. This is also required by the International Coach Federation (ICF)

Standards of Ethical Conduct and Core Coaching Competencies as follows (these are optional for non-ICF members, but highly recommended standards):

ICF Standards of Ethical Conduct:

Professional Conduct With Clients

"6) I will accurately identify my level of coaching competence and I will not overstate my qualifications, expertise or experience as a coach. 7) I will ensure that my coaching client understands the nature of coaching and the terms of the coaching agreement between us. 8) I will not intentionally mislead or make false claims about what my client will receive from the coaching process or from me as their coach. 9) I will not give my clients or any prospective clients information or advice I know to be misleading or beyond my competence. 10) I will be alert to noticing when my client is no longer benefiting from our coaching relationship and would be better served by another coach or by another resource and, at that time, I will encourage my client to make that change."

ICF Core Coaching Competencies:

1. **"Meeting Ethical Guidelines and Professional Standards -** Understanding of coaching ethics and standards and ability to apply them appropriately in all coaching situations
   a. Understands and exhibits in own behaviors the ICF Standards of Conduct (see list),
   b. Understands and follows all ICF Ethical Guidelines (see list),
   c. Clearly communicates the distinctions between coaching, consulting, psychotherapy and other support professions,
   d. Refers client to another support professional as needed, knowing when this is needed and the available resources.
2. **Establishing the Coaching Agreement -** Ability to understand what is required in the specific coaching interaction and to come to agreement with the prospective and new client about the coaching process and relationship
   a. Understands and effectively discusses with the client the guidelines and specific parameters of the coaching relationship (e.g., logistics, fees, scheduling, inclusion of others if appropriate),
   b. Reaches agreement about what is appropriate in the relationship and what is not, what is and is not being offered, and about the client's and coach's responsibilities,

   c. Determines whether there is an effective match between
   his/her coaching method and the needs of the prospective
   client." [see diagram at the end of this chapter on this point]

4. Weave a coaching approach into your presentation

Ask some coaching questions and then explain what you've done afterward to give
them a chance to experience what the coaching interaction would be like. When
they ask you for an answer, turn it around into a coaching question, e.g., "What do
you think I should do?" when asked by the prospect leads to a question by the
coach such as "It depends. What is most important to you at this career
crossroads?"

5. Qualify your client by listening before you present.

With each new prospect, we must do what is called "qualifying" by probing into
their needs and spending a substantial amount of time listening before (or
instead of) launching into a "sales spiel." Otherwise, we risk losing them before
they really have a chance to explain their needs. To do this, you might ask:

   • How quickly do you need a job?
   • Do you have severance pay? How long will it last?
   • Do you know what kind of job you want to pursue?
   • Why do you want to leave your current job?

We can then weave their language and their stated needs into our presentation
and recommendations.

6. Tailor your approach to the client's priority needs.

You may have a favorite approach or ideal process through which you would
like to take each client. For career coaches, it may be a desire to do a
comprehensive exploration of the aspects of the client's ideal work. But if a client
has just lost his/her job, this may not be the best approach to take.

Consider the following levels of needs, as outlined by psychologist Abraham
Maslow:

Maslow's Hierarchy of Needs

Physical Needs	Safety Needs	Love Needs	Self-Esteem Needs	Self-Actualization Needs
• Food/thirst • Sleep • Health • Exercise/rest • Sex • Shelter	• Security • Protection • Comfort • Peace • Order	• Acceptance • Belonging • Love/affection • Participation	• Recognition/prestige • Leadership • Achievement • Competence • Strength/intelligence	• Fulfillment of potential • Challenge • Curiosity • Creativity • Aesthetic appreciation

Consider the questions regarding the use of this model in sales in Worksheet 12 in the GEMS Workbook, and be sure to remember it in dealing with prospects.

7. *Consider the prospect's personality in your presentation.*

As a coach, it is likely that you are – or will become – familiar with one or more personality assessments. Using your knowledge of the DISC, MBTI® Assessment, or another tool of your choice, you may be able to tailor your approach based on those traits. For example, someone who is high on the "C" aspect of DiSC (Conscientious) or a clear "T" (Thinker) on the MBTI® will want more detail than someone who has an opposite preference. For more details on these instruments, see the Virtual Learning Community (member only area) at www.careercoachinstitute.com or, for MBTI® see www.cpp.com and for DISC see www.inscape.com or www.tti.com.

In addition, the client's apparent learning style (auditory, visual, kinesthetic or auditory-digital – see www.everydaysoulworks.com for details on this neurolinguistic program approach to communication) can be used to restate their needs, including those you have uncovered through your probing questions, and to show how your services will be customized to meet their unique needs. Once that match is made, the money is a secondary issue.

8. Learn and use a variety of sales techniques with your prospects.

So-called "relationship selling" has become quite popular, and one of our favorites is Reverse Selling™ as outlined in the free article "Stop Your Sales Pitch, Start Your Conversation," by Ari Galpern and available at www.reverseselling.com. This approach, simply stated, says:

> "Instead of relying on your product knowledge to spark prospect interest, try to create a conversation that focuses solely on discovering if prospective clients have a problem they want to solve and are open to considering letting you solve it. That's right -- selling is about solving your clients' problem, not about pitching them your solution. "

If you use this approach, you strive to reach agreement with the prospect on the problem to be solved; outline the reasons your current clients have purchased your service or product; tell prospects you have no idea whether your services will work for them; and ask them a question to which they can't say no.

9. Know how to address common objections to coaching.

Many coaches fear the sales process because they fear rejection. And when they hear an "objection" from the client (a reason they don't want to buy), they think they've been rejected. Wrong!

Here are some thoughts from an expert in this area:

> "A good place to begin examining the positive aspects of prospect objections is to see these objections as challenges....
>
> You should actually sometimes be optimistic when you are faced with an objection or tough question. You should see this objection simply as an indicator that you are moving either in the direction of

successfully completing the sale or in the direction of failing to make the sale.

In either case you know where you are and what you need to do in order to move ahead, course correct or break off the relationship.

You see, when a prospect voices his or her concern over a certain aspect of your product or service, **a chance has arisen for you to redirect your sales presentation.**

You now have the chance to move away from things that the prospect sees as undesirable in favor of moving towards those things that the prospect wants from you, your organization, or your product or service.

Unless the prospect's objections completely blow away your product's benefits, **you still have the opportunity to save the sale.**

Objections also give you the opportunity to hone your sales skills. The more objections that you face and successfully conquer, the better salesperson you become.

As you begin to notice patterns in the ways prospects present their objections as well as the consistent themes in these objections, **you will begin to be able to almost predict what kinds of objections your prospects will present.**

You will learn how to ask questions that help you flush them out or even eliminate them.

Knowledge leads to improvement, so knowledge involving the ways you deal with prospects' objections can only lead to improvement in your sales record, and, in turn, improvement in your income.

While objections obviously present salespeople with barriers to actually finalizing transactions, viewing these objections and tough questions in a positive light can only help you make more sales.

Objections can be seen as challenging aspects of your sales job and mastering objections can lead to an improvement in your sales performance as well as your income.

Objections may also be seen as "road maps" that point you in the right direction toward the successful completion of the sale.

Finally, these questions and objections help the salesperson to become more skilled in dealing with objections. Remember, "practice does make perfect," and the case of conquering objections is no different."

The Brooks Group, Copyright © 1998-2002, reprinted with permission; Phone: 800-633-7762

Common Objections

Following are some of the most common objections raised to coaching and suggested responses:

a) Time

Some responses to this might include "Why are you that busy?" or "That's great! I only work with people who are too busy to work with me." Or "Could we spend the first 4 sessions working on getting you ahead of your schedule?"

b) Money

Here, you might respond with "No problem, I can discount your services for the first 30/60/90 days. How much would be a reasonable amount to get started?" Or "I understand that your financial situation is tight now, but I also know that we can all find money for things we really want. How much do you want to change your work situation?"

c) I can get the help I need from my friends/family/counselor/mentor/etc.

This advice is both colored with subjectivity and worth what it costs many times (nothing!). This is the place to "strut your stuff" including credentials, certification, years of experience, and how you've successfully helped other people in similar situations.

10. Know how to close when the client is ready.

Consider this quotation from John Thrasher's "Closing the Sale," jthrasher@windsorchamber.org:

"The successful sales process will always be a derivative of building emotion. Without getting the prospect emotionally involved, the sale will never happen. **As humans, our brains tend to make final decisions using logic. It is the left hemisphere that provides humans with reasoning skills. On the other hand, it is the right hemisphere that most of the sales process must appeal to. The right hemisphere is predominately where emotion is derived from, along with imagination, music, and art.** [emphasis added]

Therefore the presentation must appeal to the right side of the brain while the close must appeal to the left. The timing of the switch is critical. It is at the peak of the emotional state that all great "closers'" know when to switch gears and make the close, so that logic is still blurred with emotion. It is probably for this reason that we are always told to "get the sale on the spot". A further complication comes from the frontal portion of the brain, the place where our past experiences or information is stored. What I might refer to as the "autopilot". The autopilot seems to activate as a back-up system. If logic is blurred with emotion, it is usually the autopilot that stops the prospect from signing on the spot. This is where closing techniques must be used with precision, timing and choice."

Knowing when to appeal to logic and when to appeal to emotion is obviously important! And when it's time to close, asking that question, "Does this sound like something you would like to do?" will open the door for the client to make a commitment.

There are three primary closing techniques, as Thrasher describes below:

One of the finest closing techniques called the **"reverse close"** uses this systematic approach. It reorganizes words to lower the prospect's defenses. If a prospect is believed to be leery of the sales pitch, their brain is already telling them to say "no" well before the close ever takes place. By using the words "do you see any reason why you would not like to join our organization" the client says "no" but indeed has said "yes" thus the name Reverse Close. Another close that still remains popular is called the **"Assumption Close".** I still to this day marvel at those who master this work of art. This close essentially takes the prospect from the sales process into the close without the prospect even realizing it. It is a smooth progression that rivals the illusion of a magic trick. In this situation the sales person really never does close. In fact, the strategy here is to not give the prospect a reason to start thinking defensively. "If they are waiting for the close to say no and it never comes they usually won't stop the process". The sales person simply goes from presenting the final feature to showing the prospect how to fill out the application and where to sign.

The final closing technique that I find useful is quite similar to the reverse close. I will call it the **"fly-fish" close.** It is where you give the client something but take it away just as fast. The strategy here is to work on their emotions. There is nothing more compelling to the emotions as the "feeling of loss." This strategy can take a number of forms such as deadlines. "Show them something really good but they only get 100% of what you just presented if they sign before a certain deadline." Organizations that use this strategy literally create programs, products and services with deadlines vs. waiting for a deadline to appear before they can use it.

How could you use these in working with your prospects?

Finally, please study the diagram on the next page to help you determine the match between you and a prospective client.

Determining The Match Between Prospect And Coach

The following diagram illustrates the process you will go through in determining whether the match is right between you and a prospective client.

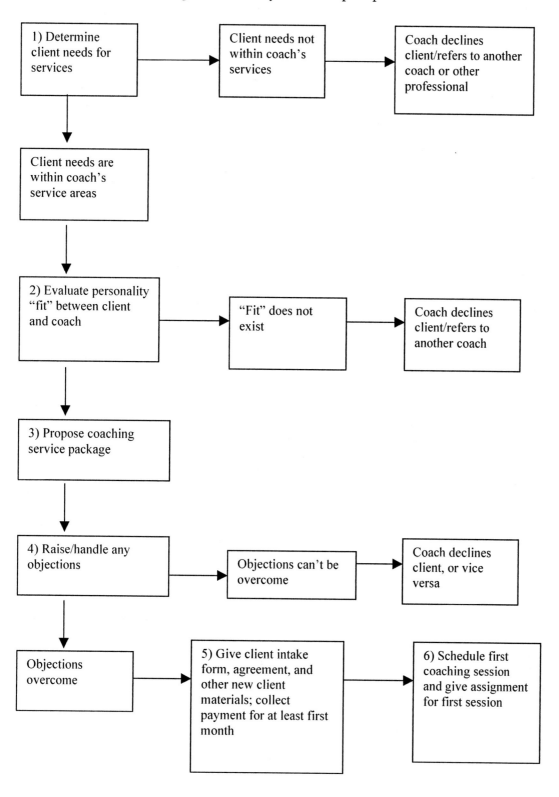

As you move through these steps, it will become increasingly clear whether the client is right for you, and vice versa.

Notes:

Please complete Exercise 12 in the GEMS Workbook now.

Epilogue

Congratulations! You now have a much clearer idea of the kind of coaching practice you want to create, and whom it will serve. And if you worked through Volume 1 of this series, *Launch Your Practice,* you also have many of the legal and administrative steps completed as well.

Volume 3, *Fill Your Practice,* will guide you through the marketing strategies that will be most effective to build a coaching practice that meets your needs both financially and emotionally. Another benefit: you will learn to generate passive income through asynchronous tools (many web-based) so that you can enjoy your life as well as your work.

THE GEMS™ SYSTEM WORKBOOK

Exercise 1: Marketing and You

Define what marketing now means to you:

What traits of Master Marketers are you going to work to develop in the coming months and years?

How much time will you plan to spend marketing:

a) in the first year of your practice?

b) in subsequent years?

Exercise 2: the GEMS™ Checklists

If you have a business now, you can use the chart below to benchmark your current marketing system (if any) and its effectiveness. Indicate 1 for "not at all true," 2 for "somewhat true," and 3 for "very true."

	Activity	Rank
1.	Position you as a one-of-a-kind brand – providing a unique service designed for one or more specific market segments	
2.	Operate 24 hours a day with minimal hands-on effort once implemented	
3.	Generate an ongoing supply of qualified leads through a variety of channels	
4.	Result in a high rate of conversion (prospects becoming customers or clients, clients becoming repeat consumers) as it moves prospects as well as existing clients up the Ladder of Trust	
5.	Encourage feedback and gather data from customers to contribute to future product enhancement/development	
6.	Enable deep penetration within all aspects of each target market via multiple media and multiple points of entry, whether individuals or organizations	
7.	Constantly be adding new contacts (via opt-in methods) to company database	
8.	Be systematized so that growth and increased volume can be managed with ease, yet personalized so that the lifetime value of each client is recognized	
9.	Leverage the Internet, email, smart auto-responders, FAQ, and other methods of technology to minimize need for hands-on activity	
10.	Result in a decreasing need for synchronous marketing time	

To track your progress through the steps of the GEMS™ system in the coming weeks (whether you are improving an existing marketing system or starting from scratch), please check each item off as it is completed.

Step in the GEMS™ System	Check when done
1. I have defined my brand, mission, business name and niche.	
2. I know who my three primary target markets are, and their needs.	
3. I have prepared a draft list of services and/or products that I believe will meet the needs of my customers in each target market.	
4. I have performed a competitive analysis of my firm vis-à-vis at least 3 competitors.	
5. I have done some market testing to test my product/service ideas with members of my prospective market groups.	
6. I have developed a multi-sensory vision statement for my business.	
7. I have determined my marketing priorities.	
8. I have created a plan that includes both direct and indirect marketing strategies, and have begun implementing it.	
9. I am using systems to track both my results and my sub-products (i.e., those activities I know will lead to the desired results).	
10. I spend time at least twice each year re-evaluating my products and services and analyzing customer feedback and sales trends, and then use this data to develop new products and services.	

Exercise 3: Statement of Abundance

My Statement of Abundance

In the space below, write the principles of money and abundance to which you consciously choose to adhere in your information business. Communicate confidence, think big, and don't be afraid to state the opposite of the self-limiting beliefs you were taught as a child!

Aggregating Your Database

Please take the following steps to begin building your database today!

1. Gather together all of those business cards you've been collecting from people at trade shows, networking events, etc.

2. List all of the people with whom you have done business in the past (if applicable) including name, email, and telephone number.

3. List friends, colleagues, vendors, customers, fellow members of sports or fitness clubs, buddies from any hobbies you have, alumni of your high school or college, and anyone else you can think of. These people may or may not be in the markets you are going to target – but they will know people in those markets!

4. If you know Excel, input those names, email addresses and phone numbers into Excel. If not, consider inputting them into Word as a database file for later mail merge; OR consider hiring a virtual assistant to do this project for you. (You might even trade this service for the service you're going to offer if you're on a shoestring budget!)

NOTE: It is not particularly important to collect physical addresses, since direct "snail" mail is expensive and no more effective than email, which is free or very low cost.

Make it your goal to gather these names together into a single database as soon as you can!

5. If you already have a web site, add a pop-up to it (use www.aweber.com or www.1shoppingcart.com or similar services) that captures the name and email address of every visitor who is interested in your services. You'll be amazed how fast your database grows this way – and everyone being added is opting into it so you do not risk being accused of spam when you do a group email!

Exercise 4: My Mission and Brand

4a. My Life's Purpose

To clarify your life purpose, find a quiet place and about an hour of undisturbed time, and respond to each of the following questions.

Clue No. 1: What do you love to do when you have spare time?

Clue No. 2: What parts of your present job or life activities do you thoroughly enjoy?

Clue No. 3: What do you naturally do well?

Clue No. 4: What have been your 10 greatest successes to date (in your eyes)?

Success	Why It's a Success for Me

Clue No. 5: Is there a cause or value or quality which you feel passionate about?

Clue No. 6: What are the 10 most important lessons you have learned in your life?

No.	Lesson
1	
2	
3	
4	
5	
6	
7	
8	
9	
10	

Clue No. 7: Think back over your life. Are there some issues or perceived problems that have occurred over and over again?

Clue No. 8: What do you daydream (or dream) about doing?

Clue No. 9: Imagine you are writing your epitaph. What things do you want to be remembered for? What things will your life be incomplete without?

Clue No. 10: What would you do if you knew you could not fail?

Now, narrow down your responses to glean the 10 most important aspects of your life purpose and write any themes you notice here:

To compose your life's purpose statement, synthesizing your responses to the Clues, use the following format:

"My life's purpose is to_____[ESSENCE]_____ through [EXPRESSION]_____."

Write your life's purpose statement here:

"My life's purpose is to _____ through _____."

4b. My Company Mission Statement

Please complete the following items as best you can with what you know now about your business mission.

My Company Mission Statement

Identity/purpose: _____ is a _____ dedicated/established to _____.

Philosophy

_____'s philosophy is _____ _____ _____

Elaborated purpose (three points)

_____ 's principal objectives or functions are:

1. _____
2. _____
3. _____

Consistency with life purpose

_____ is consistent with my life purpose in these ways:

_____

My business name: _____

4c. SWOT Analysis - Strengths, Weaknesses, Opportunities, Threats

SWOT Analysis is an effective method of identifying your Strengths and Weaknesses, and to examine the Opportunities and Threats you face, which in turn can help you clarify your brand and your UVP.   Often carrying out an analysis using the SWOT framework will be enough to reveal changes that can be usefully made. To carry out a SWOT Analysis, write down answers to the following questions:

- *Strengths:*
    - What are your advantages?
    - What do you do well?
    - What can you do better than anyone else?
    - What is natural for you?
    - What comes easy for you?
    - What are your preferences?

Consider this from your own point of view and from the point of view of the people you deal with. Don't be modest, be realistic. If you are having any difficulty with this, try writing down a list of your characteristics. Some of these will hopefully be strengths!

- *Weaknesses:*
    - What could be improved?
    - What is done badly?
    - What should be avoided?
    - What's not easy for you?

Again this should be considered from an internal and external basis - do other people perceive weaknesses that you don't see? Do your competitors do any better? It is best to be realistic now, and face any unpleasant truths as soon as possible.

- *Opportunities*
    - Where is leverage to be found?
    - Where are the good chances facing you?
    - What are the interesting trends?

Useful opportunities can come from such things as:

- Changes in technology and markets on both a broad and narrow scale
- Changes in government policy related to your field
- Changes in social patterns, population profiles, lifestyle changes
- Local Events
- New skill development
- New associations and actions taken

- *Threats*
  - What obstacles do you face?
  - What is your competition doing?
  - Are the required specifications for your job, products or services changing?
  - Is changing technology threatening your position?
  - Do you have bad debt or cash-flow problems?
  - What do you find yourself constantly up against?

SWOT Worksheet

Potential Internal Strengths	Potential Internal Weaknesses
1.	1.
2.	2.
3.	3.
4.	4.
5.	5.
6.	6.
7.	7.
8.	8.
9.	9.
10.	10.

Potential External Opportunities	Potential External Threats
1.	1.
2.	2.
3.	3.
4.	4.
5.	5.
6.	6.
7.	7.
8.	8.
9.	9.
10.	10.

Exercise 5: My Target Markets

Target Market 1:
  a)   **Demographic customer profile.**

Describing your customers using the following factors will give you a profile of their key characteristics for use in your marketing program.

If your customers are individuals in the general public:
  Sex: M   F
  Marital status: S   M   D   W
  Age range: _____
  Number of children: _____
  Religion: _____
  Race(s): _____
  Lifestyle, activities, hobbies: _____

_____

If you sell primarily to other businesses:
  Size: _____ (by gross annual sales or other measure)
  Number of employees: _____
  Annual gross income: $_____
  Age of business: _____
  Industry(ies): _____
  Location(s): _____
  Buyer/Decision maker within organization (title): _____
  Other   similar   characteristics:

_____
_____

  b)   **Psychographics**

    What do you know about the preferences of your pattern from a psychological standpoint? _____

    Magazines my ideal clients read: _____

    Industry   associations   my   ideal   clients   are   involved   in:
_____

    Television shows my clients watch: _____

Stores in which my ideal clients shop: _____

Other psychographic information: _____

c)   Customer population projection

To do accurate sales projections, you must determine how many potential customers lie within your geographic market.

What is your geographic market (Portland Metro area, state of Oregon, other states, U.S., Pacific Rim, worldwide, etc.)?

_____

_____

Consult census data, demographic profiles from your local newspaper or other sources, trade associations, and other resources in your local library and internet to determine how many of the customers fitting the demographic profile you have defined lie within your geographic market.   Write your conclusions here:

_____

_____

_____

Does your research indicate that this number will grow during the coming years? Why or why not?

_____

How many purchases do you estimate an average customer will make from you each year? _____

Of what product(s) or service(s)? At what price?

_____

_____

What types of customers will buy more than one of your products or services?_____

Repeat this process with each target market.

My Target Markets:

	Description	Economic Cycle
Market 1		
Market 2		
Market 3		

Exercise 6: Product Mix

1. What do you currently offer (or plan to offer) as your coaching services? Examples: "life purpose coaching – 1, 8, or 12 sessions"; "job search coaching – with or without a resume, with or without interview, lengths ranging from 1-3 months." Don't forget sponsorship of a job search networking-group (physical meeting or via teleconference) as an option! Write your planned services below, remembering the principle of offering each client three alternatives:

Service No. 1: _____
_____
_____
_____

Service No. 2: _____
_____
_____
_____

Service No. 3: _____
_____
_____
_____

What products would you like to develop? List ideas below (remember, they're just ideas – let your imagination run here!):

Books and workbooks:

CD's:

Classes/seminars/speech topics:

Web-based assessments or other tools:

Other:

How could these products fit within your service options above?

Exercise 7: Competitors

In the space below, list the businesses you consider to be your major competitors. Next to each, designate which of the three types they are -- a, b, or c. (See chapter 7 for explanation.)

MY COMPETITORS

Competitor Name	Type
1.	
2.	
3.	
4.	
5.	
6.	
7.	
8.	
9.	
10.	

Next, number your **three key competitors** with a 1, 2, and 3 by their name above. Now rank each of your three key competitors by doing a detailed inquiry into their business and how they do it. Rank them as 1 (poor), 2 (adequate) or 3 (excellent).

RANKING MY COMPETITORS

Factor	My Business	#1	#2	#3
Advertising, promotion				
Appearance				
Credit policy				
Customer service				
Experience/expertise/credentials				
Image/reputation				
Length of time in business				
Location				
Management/organization				
Pricing				
Product quality				
Product selection/mix				
Reliability				

Sales methods				
Use of space/staff				
Web site appeal				
OVERALL RANKING				

Based on your survey, what percentage of the possible customers in your geographic market do you estimate will buy from you and from each of your competitors?

> My business: __%
> Competitor 1:__%
> Competitor 2:__%
> Competitor 3:
> (Total must equal 100%)

Some changes I could make to my product, service, distribution, or other aspects of my business to improve my competitive position are:

Exercise 8: Market Testing

How will you test the product and service ideas you have generated for viability? List your ideas below:

Are you planning to do a survey? List the questions you plan to include below. Ask yourself: what do I need to know about my clients' hot buttons and needs in order to best target this product or service to meet those needs?

Exercise 9: Marketing Mistakes

Which of the following mistakes have you made so far in your business?

MISTAKE	Yes	No
Thinking Small - Marketing is for Big Business, not me		
Thinking of marketing as an expense, when it is an investment		
Engaging in marketing activities only when business is down		
Performing little or no market research		
Failure to differentiate your business from your competition		
Failure to segment and target the market		
Inadequate branding		
Competing with the competition		
Thinking of sales, not profits!		
Losing focus - expanding too early or unnecessarily		

What is your plan to remedy the area in which the mistake was made?

Exercise 10: Vision

Please write your vision of your business, first in the short-term (the next 6 months) and second in the long-term (1-2 years out) in the most vivid, sensory, explicit terms you can. Think big! As Goethe said, "*Whatever you can do, or dream you can, begin it. Boldness has genius, power, and magic in it. Begin it now.*"

My 6-month vision:

My 1-year vision:

Check what you have written. Does it meet the criteria discussed in the chapter:
   a) be written in the present tense
   b) be open-ended,
   c) be sufficiently specific so that you can recognize it when you see it – (it balances the two);
   d) stretch your rational mind's beliefs about what is possible for you; and
   e) focus on the feelings you will experience as the vision materializes.

Exercise 11: Law of Attraction

What are your biggest challenges in:

- Earning income?
- Attracting clients?
- Keeping clients?
- Filling your practice?

List them here:

Now, review the three principles of the Law of Attraction in chapter 11. How might they apply here?

What could you do to begin changing these circumstances for the better, using the Attraction principles? List at least two steps here:

Exercise 12: Sales Strategies

In honing your ability to be effective in converting prospects to clients, you will need to work with all 10 ideas on "Coach as Salesperson" described in Chapter 12. Assess your comfort level with each in the table below, using "1" for "not comfortable," "2" for "somewhat comfortable" and "3" for "very comfortable."

Skill	Comfort Level
1. Under promise, over deliver	
2. Have at least 3 levels of service to offer, with respective fee levels	
3. Clearly state what coaching is, and isn't	
4. Weave a coaching approach into your presentation	
5. Qualify your client by listening before you present.	
6. Tailor your approach to the client's priority needs.	
7. Consider the prospect's personality in your presentation.	
8. Learn and use a variety of sales techniques with your prospects.	
9. Know how to address common objections to coaching.	
10. Know how to close when the client is ready.	

Applying Maslow's Hierarchy of Needs to Sales

When using Maslow's Hierarchy on page 67 with prospects, you will want to consider asking them these questions:

1. What level is the client at now?
2. How would you use Maslow's hierarchy to coach him/her?

Let's apply this in a couple of hypothetical case studies:

Example 1: Your client, Jane, comes to you feeling dissatisfied with her job. As you begin working with her, you discover that she is overextended financially and can barely make ends met. Yet she really wants to make a career change and increase her level of fulfillment at work.

Example 2: Another client, Joe, has just been laid off from his long-time job. Because of the recent boom times, he has acted out the stereotype of the "last of the red hot spenders," spending everything he made and more, and not saving. Now he's out of work, not sure what to do next, and supporting his family (including two small children) is his number 1 priority.

What is the likely reaction of these clients if you present the Authentic Vocation model to them and suggest they explore their life purpose?

Why would they react that way?

As a coach, what would the best course of action be with these clients?

The best course of action in many cases in which the client's financial needs overshadow his/her desire to explore ideal work is to take a two-part approach to career coaching. First, help the client achieve a job that will pay the bills but will not take 100% (or more!) of his/her time and energy. Then, once the financial pressure is relieved, the client can continue working with you to clarify his/her Authentic Vocation™ and conduct a search in his/her spare time while working at the transitional job.

ABOUT MARCIA BENCH

Marcia Bench is the Founder and Director of Career Coach Institute. A Master Certified Career Coach™ and nationally respected expert in the job/career transition field, she has been coaching and consulting both individual and corporate clients since 1986.

A former attorney, Marcia has authored 10 books, including the forthcoming *Career Coaching: An Insider's Guide* (Davies-Black November 2003), *Thriving in Transition* (Simon & Schuster) and *When 9 to 5 Isn't Enough* (Hay House) and has been a featured speaker/trainer at over 400 local, regional and national conferences, as well as a guest on numerous television and radio programs. Her mission is to help individuals and organizations identify and implement their highest vision to reach their potential.

Marcia's coaching experience includes work with managers and executives from such firms as Qualcomm, Intel, Intuit, Kelloggs, FedEx, Westinghouse, Willamette Industries, Raytheon, US West, Shell, PetCo, and Kimberly Clark, among others, as well as dozens of business owners, professionals, and military officers entering the civilian workforce.

She was a Senior Vice President in a dot-com career management firm for 4 years, and previously spent 10 years as President of New Work Directions, a business and consulting firm she founded. Ms. Bench developed her expertise in business start-up and management in part through her 4 years as a practicing attorney specializing in business and employment issues.

Marcia was founder and charter president of the Portland (Oregon) Metro Chapter of the Association of Career Professionals International. She is a current member of the International Coach Federation and the Association of Career Professionals International.

Marcia's education includes a Juris Doctorate from Northwestern School of Law of Lewis & Clark College and a Bachelor of Science in Psychology from Western Oregon University. In addition, she is a Certified Career Management Practitioner through the Institute of Career Certification International, a Certified Business Coach, a Certified Teleleader and Master Certified Career Coach.

Career Coach Institute, LLC and High Flight Press (Publisher)
P.O. Box 5778, Lake Havasu City, AZ 86404
Phone: 928-764-2870   Fax: 208-692-0574
coach@careercoachinstitute.com
www.careercoachinstitute.com

High Flight Press

PRODUCT CATALOG (All by Marcia Bench, MCCC)

Career Coaching

Career Coaching: An Insider's Guide (hard cover)	$34.95

A step-by-step roadmap to helping clients discover their Authentic Vocation,™ using QuantumShift!™ coaching techniques to get fast results.   Also includes Career Coach's Toolbox.

Study Guide for Independent Career Coaches	$24.95
Coming fall 2003: *Study Guide for Internal Career Coaches*	$24.95
Audio Lectures CD's (27 lectures to accompany textbook on 4 CD's)	$99.95
Coaching Demonstration CD's (12 coaching demo's illustrating concepts in text)	$39.95

NOTE: All of the above products are included in CCI's career coach training and certification; see details at <u>www.careercoachinstitute.com</u>

Practice-Building for Coaches Series

Launch Your Practice	$18.95

This nuts-and-bolts manual leads you through the maze of requirements for starting your own coaching practice, including how to choose and register your business and domain name, whether to incorporate, where to find financing, contract forms, merchant accounts, web resources, bookkeeping, and more.

Discover Your Niche	$18.95

Are you a new coach struggling to decide what kind of coaching practice you want to build? Or what to name your business and your web site? You'll discover how to do this and much more.

Fill Your Practice	$18.95

If you are a new or established coach who is dedicated to being successful, you know you need to market. Learn how to use the internet to build passive income streams and drive clients to you.

Job Search/Career Design Series

Discover Your Authentic Vocation	$14.95

Contains exercises to help you gain clarity about your career direction, create your ideal job, and make changes in your life.

Turbo-Charge Your Job Search	$14.95

If you're looking for a new job, you don't want to be without this guide to the practical side of job search. Learn about resumes, interviewing, networking, negotiating, and more.

Transition Management

Thriving in Transition: Effective Living in Times of Change (trade paper)	$11.95

If you're facing increasing changes in your life, this book is for you. It outlines the Thriver Profile -- traits shared by those who thrive during transition. Includes roadmap of transition process.

Don't Survive – Thrive *in Transition*	$14.95

A workbook to help you implement the Thriver approach to transitions, with lots of "fill-in-the-blanks" exercises and useful lists of tips and strategies to make change work for you.

Ask us about our turnkey outplacement program, now available for licensing!

HIGH FLIGHT PRESS PRODUCT ORDER FORM

Name	
Company	
Street Address (for billing)	
City, State ZIP	
Street Address (for shipment – if different)	
City, State ZIP	
Home Telephone	
Work Telephone	
Email address (to send receipt)	
CASH ORDERS We take e-checks!	
	ABA Routing No.:
	Bank Account No.:
CREDIT CARD ORDERS	
Card number:	
Expiration date:	
Name on card:	
Signature (to authorize purchase)	
PRODUCTS DESIRED	

Quantity	Product Name	Price Each	Total Price
	Subtotal		
	Shipping & handling (20% of total)		
	TOTAL DUE		

Allow 7-10 business days for processing

For More Information, email us: coach@careercoachinstitute.com www.careercoachinstitute.com
High Flight Press • PO Box 5778 • Lake Havasu City, AZ 86403 • 1-866-CCOACH-4

Printed in the United States
1393500001B/1-14